THE

BIG 3.0

LIFE NUGGETS YOU NEED TO KNOW BEFORE YOU ARE 30

SOLOMON OJEAGBASE

WITH

CHARLES UMEH

outskirts
press

Table of Contents

Dedication

To my Dad, Dr. Sunny Emmanuel Ojeagbase on the occasion of his 70th birthday celebration. Thank you for running so I can fly. I wish you many more fruitful and flourishing years in good health and a sound mind.

Appreciation

First and foremost, my gratitude and reverence goes to God Almighty the creator of the universe and all that dwell in it, for giving me the inspiration. It's a privilege and I am thankful to have been given the opportunity.

My parents Dr. Sunny Emmanuel and Pastor Mrs. Esther Ojeagbase, you have been strong figures in my life, my first role models and you both have left an indelible mark in me. I am unable to quantify your contribution to my growth in my journey to adult-hood. I am thankful for the love, prayers and care you continually show to me and my family.

Olatomiwa my beautiful wife, you have been a con-stant source of inspiration and encouragement to me, the mother to my lovely kids Hadassah and Havilah, who always put a smile on my face whenever I think about them. My love for you knows no bounds - it's a blessing to be walking this life's path with you.

I have been blessed with wonderful, siblings Justina (Funmi), Julius, Stella (rest her soul), Rachel, Blessing last but not least Samson. You have all been very influential and have played a role in some way in my life's journey. The pandemic has brought us even closer. I cherish the moments we spend together via Zoom - the cord of love that binds us together will only get stronger.

My mother-in law Deaconess Shade Ariran, Grandma as my daughter fondly calls her. I appreciate your prayers and show of love towards my family. Not forgetting my brothers and sister in-law Seun, Moji, Tobi, Fola and Bolu; you guys rock!

Two very important members of my extended family, my uncle John and aunty Lydia, very supportive and caring for the family at large there is no comparing, you are the best. My cousins Feyikemi, Eniola, Joshua, Jessica, Tioluwa, Deborah, Sandra, Endurance - my closest friends.

I have been blessed to have very wonderful teachers who have made profound impact on me, some of who are; Mr. Oke, my English teacher at my alma mater Home Sciences Association Secondary School (H.A.S.S.S), who always had my back and saw to it that I became Social prefect against all odds. Dr. Mrs.

Fayomi from the Department of Policy and Strategic Studies at Covenant University, who encouraged me through my university days and even now, still encourages me to attend Model United Nations (MUN) conferences.

This book would not have been written without the experience I got working under certain people who guided me during my naïve years in business, Alhaji Mumini Alao, the Group Managing Director of Complete Communications Limited, who has been a friend of the family for many years. He always makes time off his busy schedule to read my proposals and advise on business decisions. Ehi Braimah who is the Publisher/Editor-in-Chief of Naija Times and President of Rotary Club Victoria Island chapter, Honourable Larry Aghedo, former Commissioner for Economic Planning and Budget in Edo State, Dror Harazi my Israeli friend, who is always a supporter of my business ideas, and Charles Umeh the co-Author of this book. We cliqued the first day we met and have helped each other grow since them.

I would also like to express my gratitude to my friends Sola Ojo, Damola Almaroof, Ezuma Okoronkwo, Bukky Orenuga, Ibrahim Yaradua, Ibrahim Bawa, Victor Chiwuzor, Ayo Agunbiade, Afolabi Ogunde and Ekene Blessed. You guys have proved to be true friends with good ideals, you lot have rubbed off on me positively.

The 2015/2016 set of Lagos Business School, EMBA20, especially members of Group 2. Our WhatsApp group is an encyclopedia of learning, a constant information sharing tool which has been very helpful in my business and personal life.

Similarly, members of International Business Resource centre (IBRC) class of 2016; making that business trip to the United States as a group was an eye opener for me and our subsequent meetings have been a source of constant energy for me to push the limits in my business endeavours.

This book will not be complete without acknowledging my colleagues at Complete Sports who I regard as members of my family. Also not forgetting my business partners and Clients. Your dedication and hard work can be seen in the success we have achieved as a team. We have worked together for years and I hope we will continue to strive to be better while creating innovative services to meet the needs of an ever evolving world.

Finally, my appreciation goes to everyone and anyone who has made an impression in my life but was not mentioned as at the time of writing this chapter. Always know that you are deeply appreciated.

#Thank you

Introduction

Writing a book has always been on my bucket list. It is one of the few things I believe I owe to my creator. I believe that having come thus far in life, God has blessed me with the wisdom to be able to conceptualize, compartmentalize and harmonize my thoughts and experiences in the form of a book.

There is no doubt in me that the lessons and knowledge gained on my journey are profound. I am a firm believer that all things work together for good, for those who love God and are called according to His purpose.

If I had not been privileged to have these experiences on my journey, I would not be in a position to write this book, which I hope will be a source of inspiration and a manual of sorts for teenagers and youths who look up to me as a role model.

Our sole aim in writing this short book is to inspire, inform, and encourage. Ultimately, we hope to be able to make it clear from experience that delay is not complete denial. With the right attitude and mindset we can always excel as long as we are ready to stretch our minds.

It is important we state that this is not a religious book either. While writing, references were made to some passages of the Holy Bible without quoting the verse to make it easy for non-Christians.

As said earlier, this is to inspire, inform and encourage teenagers and youths alike and not to prove the superiority of any religion. It is also not a case of – like they say – another "inspire to aspire to acquire book".

Instead, our focus is on your mind and sharing thoughts and experiences that helped us. So for clarity, the book would have two sections the first is my voice the second is Charles' illustration of my thoughts which is expressed as INSIGHTS.

First Things First

I wake up every morning looking to the heavens and confessing 'this is the day the Lord has made, I will rejoice and be glad in it'. You may call it my morning ritual and you will be right; however, I regard it as putting my better foot forward as an expression of my daily gratitude to God Almighty.

Not everyone believes in God, but I challenge any atheist to hold his or her breath for one minute and let us see how long you exist. I bet you would feel a terrible sinking feeling, right? Then my response would be if you have held your breath for a little longer what would have happened? The clear fact is that there is a supreme being who created the oxygen we breathe free of charge to keep us alive.

I believe it is a privilege to be born into a Christian family. In addition, the teachings have rubbed off on my life; its impact is tremendous. From my point of view, the Bible is an encyclopedia of every event and circumstance I will ever encounter in my lifetime - it has all it takes to have my needs met.

In the course of this book, I will be letting you in on some of these passages to elaborate on some points. It is important that you always make it a point of duty to acknowledge your Maker and invite Him to guide you in everything you do. *"This Book of the Law shall not depart from your mouth, but you shall meditate in it day and night, that you may observe to do according to all that is written in it. For then you will make your way prosperous, and then you will have good success"* gives a good account of our responsibility regarding this point.

Insight

As humans, it is super clear that there is a void we all have, that needs to be filled by God. Come to think of it: the very best of us go to bed at night and never have a clue of what happens when our eyes are shut and in a different world. I believe it's extremely foolish to think we possibly wake up at the jolt of our alarm clock or our getting used to our body. The fact remains that we exist and are controlled by a supreme being. Religion calls it God, some schools of thought call it the universe but in all, gratitude sets us off on a different path and reminds us we exist because we were given a new opportunity to be. I believe waking up with this mindset every day is enough motivation to drive us to give life our best shot and make everyone whose effort to keep us alive and going, worth it.

It's best to start with gratitude to God for counting us worthy to be alive against all odds, our caregivers or parents for molding our minds and shaping our life, our siblings, loved ones, and peers for their support. Popular media mogul, Oprah Winfrey has a recommended gratitude routine known as "gratitude journaling" which involves writing down the things you are grateful for and reading them to yourself. It is important that you consider the very little things while writing this list and let it be your reminder of how much you do have before you start your day and when you end it. I also recommend this to you.

The goal of this exercise is in who you become. When you always realize you are more than just you and are a part of a very big thing, it broadens your understanding. Always make it a routine to count your blessings and just in case you think life has been too unfair to you and you have nothing to be grateful for, look back at that list and be kind to yourself.

CHAPTER **2**

Know What You Want Out of Life

Know what you want out of life. Write the vision down and make it plain

It is one thing to have a dream; it is another thing to know whether the dream is feasible, looking at the circumstances that border around the dream. For example, you cannot dream to be the next American president without first being a citizen of the United States of America. Likewise, you cannot hope to become the president of Nigeria without holding a senior secondary school certificate. Don't misquote me, God does work in mysterious ways, His thoughts are not our thoughts neither are His ways ours, but there is a billion to one chance that you will achieve these two ambitions without first ticking the eligibility boxes. So let's check these boxes while we continue on our journey.

Living your life to probabilistic wandering is likened to when you have a dream of becoming something you are not equipped for. This can be juxtaposed to winning the lottery. The statistics actually have it that no lottery winner has ever stayed wealthy after receiving their winnings. They most likely squander it in the first three years of receiving the money or less. This is not how you want to live your life I guess?

Your dreams have to be SMART. As a student of the social era, you should be ready to learn from YouTube what the SMART principle is all about if it's new to you.

Let me share a bit of my journey with you. I graduated from Covenant University, Nigeria in 2007, and was posted to Kaduna in Northern Nigeria for my mandatory National Youth Service Corps. While at work one day, a friend in the United Kingdom sent me an invite on Facebook. I was working at MDS logistics which was a subsidiary of UAC (United African Company) at the time. That fateful afternoon, I saw the friend request, accepted it and went on to browse the website. It immediately dawned on me how revolutionary this social network could be in the future. Looking back, I was not wrong.

Prior to joining MDS logistics, the regional manager during my interview asked me a clear question on what areas I would contribute to the company's growth seeing that they were a logistic company and I studied International Relations in the university. At that time I did not have an answer to that question, so I did a research on the history of Facebook and found the platform was developed by a young adult like myself and then an eureka moment lit a bulb in my head. I thought about the possibility of trying my hands on Information Technology (IT). The thought of doing this consumed me that I determined to do something about it. That was my inspiration.

Long story short, I later got a partial scholarship to study Oracle Database Management at NIIT in Kaduna Northern Nigeria and ultimately went on to study Business Information Technology at Kingston University in London. I have been in the tech space ever since then and have never for one day regretted my choice and my decision.

Insight

We live in an era where the power of the space we live in rivals several generations behind us. This is the power of the space we live in and the power of friendships being developed especially on the digital space. With the birth of Facebook by Mark Zuckerberg and other social media platforms, no doubt, friendships have been revolutionized and partnerships have taken a new dive. The best connections cannot only be found in clubs or bars but also on social media streets like Facebook, WhatsApp, Twitter, Instagram and others which are still big deals for us in 2020.

The best of us become valuable by sharing, helping and making the best of the connections.

Social media is a tool and is designed to help us explore and expose our likes or curation of what we wish to do. For instance, my social media pages sometimes serve as my vision boards, as I share what I plan to do. And most times when I do them, I owe it as a duty to tell others about it, and this builds credibility. In addition, doing this helps showcase our gifts or exchange skills, opportunity for value, and bridge the location gap which circumstances have put on our path. I believe that in the first five minutes of looking at your page and space, anyone should be able to put a picture to what you do, what you can bring to their table and figure out if it connects to their journey and path. The onus mostly lies on you to make sure social media is your tool and well maximized and you aren't just the tool.

Always go back to your page to review its contents and ask if this version of you is one you are proud of and keep tweaking as you evolve and in all be truthful to you.

In this era of change and continuous evolving, we simply make more connections. Gone are the days when you hear things like: Do not enter vehicles with strangers. There are now quick ride-hailing companies – such as Lift, Uber and Bolt, conveying people to their destinations once they make a trip request at the click of a button on their phones.

Do not open your house to strangers: Airbnb services are helping people put up their spaces for a fee for people looking for comfortable homestays, lodging and tourism experiences.

The best storytellers in the new career path we call influencer marketing carved their path on the spotlight because of the influence they made on their social media space. Hence, it is advised that you make sure you do not sell yourself short in this era with what you put out on social media. These days some Embassies request your social media account during your visa application interview. The reason being that it is easy to spot people's interests with their online behaviours. While you bask in the euphoria of using these tools, always ask yourself before you post your content; 'what if this is played on the 9'O clock news on national TV?' Would you be proud of what you let everyone see? It is great to sound "woke" and take sides during online controversies; however, always make sure the tools of this era work in your favor through what you do with it.

Be known for something and do not be that random

person. People have got jobs, closed business deals, made meaningful connections and exchanged values with these tools you take for granted; so make the best of it and always ask yourself if your actions are helping you be better or otherwise.

In all you do online just be aware that the internet never forgets, especially those who live on a certain street called Twitter. Don't give people the power to bully you because of your actions in the past, let your digital footprint work for you.

CHAPTER 3

Go to School but Leave Early

Education is the surest way to success. Our fathers and mothers were able to get lush jobs that paid fat salaries with benefits because of their possession of a school-leaving certificate. There was a relatively low literacy rate and inflation was minimal or nonexistent in those days. Fast forward to these days and you would see that this is not the case. I read an article some time ago where a gentleman lamented that he graduated from the prestigious Corona School Lagos (for those who are familiar with the city of Lagos, Corona is one of the crème- de-la-crème schools in the city) but he couldn't afford to enroll his own kids to go to this school in recent times, even though he was earning relatively the same amount of money his parents earned when they enrolled him to the same school years ago. But no doubt with the years' difference, inflation occurred and things that made sense then aren't the same in 2020.

This should already tell you that times have changed and only the very fittest would survive. Most technology companies I know do not hire people based on certificates; rather, they do so based on the number of deliverables you can complete within a stipulated period. Education has its place in society. However, if your desire is to be financially free, then, by all means, start reading and learning from practical books on Financial Literacy and how to make the right investments.

As mentioned earlier, education has its place in society. It gives you a sense of worth and belonging, as you are perceived as a refined or polished member of the society when you have one. There are places an educated person has access to which is out of bounds for a person who has little or no education. At times, the difference between the educated and the uneducated can be spotted without having to look through each person's certificate. Your carriage and composure sets you apart. Education gives you the key to have a certain level of confidence and courage. So as long as you are young, do all you can to invest in it.

Insight

Early in 2019, news broke out on how companies like Apple, Google, and Netflix (all new generation tech companies) removed the policy that made recruitment only open to employees with a degree. With this, the focus is more on what the employees are bringing to the table in an evolving world, where your skill sets are not normally taught in schools but learnt outside school, obviously because of obsolete curriculums. No doubt it gives more opportunity to the next young person seeking to get into the work force, to focus more on skills and be great at one or several. Having a Hybrid skillset is fast becoming the new culture and you shouldn't close your eyes to it.

There were several conversations on how this could become industry norms in the nearest future, thereby making it an alibi for young people to refuse to go to school. My opinion on this is simple, get a good education and arm yourself with skills and be great at it. True as this sounds, the story is obviously incomplete with the narrative "you don't need to go to school to succeed". We should be cautious of passing this message to the next generation because the consequences could be calamitous.

Going to school helps in building our character, affords us the mindset to explore opportunities with peers, teaches us how to manage and understand people from diverse environments, and in the end, if we are lucky, we become prepared for the new world outside of school. You need more financial intelligence to sustain wealth; hence it is recommended that creatives and passion-driven individuals learn the business aspect of every craft they practice. In as much as we all want a new era without degrees, humans must learn the basics of how to manage money, the magic of compound interest and how money works in general. No matter how much you hate mathematics (if you do), it waits for you in real life, because you must know your numbers, else you will always be at the mercy of those who do.

CHAPTER 4

No Knowledge Is Lost

This is a sequel to the previous chapter. There is a clear distinction between education and experience or what is called 'Being hands-on'. This distinction has made many business people conclude that education is overrated. They argue that people shouldn't waste their time sitting in a classroom and listening to a teacher who can barely send his or her child(ren) to school. Although this is somewhat accurate, there are informal skills and experiences we gain by merely interacting with others in a classroom environment. At school, we learn from our teachers, lecturers, facilitators and even the driver that takes us to school every morning. This may sound awkward, but I learned to drive by studying my dad's driver each time we went out.

One day, my high school friend came visiting and we decided to leave the house. We drove to

Victoria Island (which was about 25 kilometers) from where my parents lived at that time. I was just 16 years old and was home for the Christmas break from the university. It was the era where mobile phones just came into vogue and only a few school kids had mobile phones. My dad would have called me to insist that I stayed where I was while he sent someone to come drive me back. Fortunately, I didn't have a mobile phone, so I drove back home in one piece, and that was the day my dad concluded that I had to go get a temporary driving license.

Never look down on anyone or any knowledge coming from anyone. You can never know it all. Learning in bits and pieces can give you an edge.

Insight

Oftentimes we underestimate the power of observation, listening, and picking up skills gained from shadowing people who are ahead of us or have skills we would like to have. I once asked an audience I was speaking to how many of them were taught how to sign their signature. Very few agreed to have been taught. What this meant was that we probably winged it because it is believed you should know. Asides having the skills, it is always best to be in the right place and right environment that gives you an opportunity to blossom. Irrespective of how the world keeps changing, it is best to be a fulltime student and develop a sponge mindset by listening more and talking less.

There is a business practice called apprenticeship, which allows young aspiring business owners to work under a boss for a particular length of time. The goal is to understudy the Master while absorbing all you need to learn, including the discipline involved. In the long run, the apprentice is expected to become a better version of their Master, set up their own practice and continue the cycle of recruiting more apprentices under them which in the long term breeds more informal schooled business rookies.

This singular practice of apprenticeship could always be applied in every field we embark on. The apprentice is not in a hurry to be like his master. Rather, he explores the luxury of learning from everyone during his time and no knowledge is lost on him. Be an apprentice of books and great people. Watch educational videos on YouTube, feed yourself with great mind foods. In the end, the preparatory stage of learning which is often difficult, always paves way for us to be better in the long term.

CHAPTER 5

Make Friends as Fast as You Lose Them

My mum once gave me a book to read in my early teens, titled: "How to win friends and influence people" by Dale Carnegie. Knowing what I know today, that title is so much of a contrast. You cannot try to win a friend and influence him or her at the same time. Winning friends would mean making yourself to be seen as compatible, doing things your friends are akin to just to get their attention or approval. By so doing, they are influencing you and not the other way around. Just imagine if the person you are imitating is a heavy substance abuser! Many teenagers and youths alike have fallen prey to the wrong people in a bid to fit in.

One day worth remembering, was the day a friend of mine came visiting. My dad told me when he got into the house that he never wanted to see any of my friends who wears an earring, in his house.

Apparently, my dad, on his way into the house, had spotted a young lad wearing an earring. He asked the security personnel who he was looking for and he replied he was looking for me. I was not aware prior to that encounter that I had a visitor but on meeting my dad to welcome him home, he informed me of my guest. As I stepped outside, I saw my friend brandishing an earring on his left ear. At that time, magnetic earrings (studs) were a popular fashion accessory for teenagers.

I immediately told him that if he wanted to come into the house, he would have to remove the studs. I did not mention to him that my dad had scolded me, as that would sour his mood. I hope you get me. What I am driving at is simply to be the influencer and make sure you always lead the right path. In essence; make the brand, do not let the brand make you.

Insight

The impact of friendships and how they rub off can never be overemphasized. The best of friends rub off on us, likewise the worst. Time reveals the effect of friendship. I believe sometimes, while growing up, we really don't know what's good for us, and that explains why we tilt towards trends that are fickle and temporary. If we are lucky to have parents or guardians who keep us accountable and who know who we are, they sometimes demand more from us and our association, because they understand the effect of friendship.

An example of the effect of friendship could also be traceable to the story of how Facebook founder, Mark Zuckerberg, met with five of his close friends, during the build-up to the platform that birthed what we know today as Facebook. Only two of the invited friends showed up. They are Dustin Moskovitz and Eduador, and they would later become the first beneficiaries to the wealth of the company, just for the simple reason that they showed up and rubbed off their friend's genius. Looking back, their success was simply as a result of their friendship to a rookie Facebook founder. It is great to aspire to be a friend of Zuk; it is also great to be a Zuckerberg and honour your friendship with people and serve the world with your gifting.

.

CHAPTER 6

Dare to Be Different

Many of us claim to be different, unique and special but daily we contradict ourselves by letting the cares of this world influence our mood, attitude, and behaviors. What made the biblical Daniel stand out? He did not eat the king's meal as was the custom of the time. What made Joseph stand out? He was a dreamer, morally disciplined and interpreted Pharaoh's dream. How about Moses? He refused to be addressed as an Egyptian and chose to follow the leading of God despite all odds. If we must stand out, we must choose to do those things that are often uncomfortable and distinguish us from the crowd.

I have always sought to standout, not in an arrogant way but by living simply. A friends once told me "To be simple is not simple". I have sought to simplify my life to the extent that I seldom worry about what most people worry about. That is not living in denial because those cares exist, however I have made a conscious effort to live simply, I have the mindset that anything I don't have I don't need.

While at the University I did not have a clique, I was friends with everybody, I can't even remember if I had enemies. My dressing, walking, and talking were unique to me. I was popular even though I didn't have the latest of everything. Even till this day, people still call me by my nickname. It stuck because I was good at being me. I achieved this level of popularity because I decided to focus on what I had going for me rather than what was going wrong with me.

We cannot claim to be different and still be making careless personal decisions.

Insight

To be different in this current era and age, there is a price to pay. In addition, I hope you understand it has been like that, even before you were born, and would remain the same as the world keeps evolving. Being different would require us most times, to be mocked and looked down on as lesser humans. However, from someone who has lived your age and had friends like you, I would simply request you make it a duty to understand your uniqueness and embrace it. With the constant fear of missing out (FOMO), many young people wish to become people they are not for the sake of sounding cool or trendy. We all love people who can be trusted. Even a thief wishes to keep his money with someone who is likely not in his line of trade. This clearly should show why you must stand out from the crowd in every aspect of your life and become your true self.

The story was told of how a certain organization overseas was hiring, and the head of Human Resources had the mandate to fill a vacancy within a time frame. The criterion was simply that they wanted an African in their firm to portray a rainbow culture which was part of the company's value and culture. The only reason someone got that job was simply that they were qualified and that they were African by birth because that was the only piece left for their puzzle. The company was so excited to make the right hire when they found the match.

When society pressures you into wanting to be like everyone else, take pleasure in your difference and remind yourself, you're the best version of yourself as long as you keep improving and working on you. If there is any lesson on the subject of uniqueness that sticks well, do well to read this book carefully, get the perspectives from our inputs and explore the gift of collaboration we bring to you. Our difference makes us unique. We can't be like the next person but we believe our uniqueness when harnessed can be limitless.

CHAPTER 7

Early to Bed, Early to Rise

I remember growing up in the city of Lagos, Nigeria with my parents. After a busy day they would unwind by watching a popular soap opera that aired on NTA (Nigerian Television Authority) titled "Checkmate". Just before the program aired, my parents would ask us kids to go to bed as we had to be up early for school the next morning. This used to upset me a lot, and I always looked forward to the day I'd be able to go to bed anytime I wanted and wake up anytime I liked.

However, knowing what I know now, I would simply say to you: GROWING UP IS A TRAP! Don't be in a hurry to grow up. Successful people go to bed late and wake up early. I can speak for myself because this has been my experience so far in my short stay here on earth. I advise you make it a habit by starting out to practice it.

Some may argue that I am not successful; however, that is an argument for another lifetime. I did not write this book as proof that I am successful, but to prove to myself that I can make an impact without holding a public office and that's what I want you to take from this. That's what I want you to see, most brilliant ideas don't come during the hustle and bustle of the day, rather in the cool of the night. If you are spiritual, you will know that the early mornings is a better time to take charge of your day. Timing is everything in life, and God has graciously given every one of us the same 24 hours. What we do with that time is our responsibility.

Insight

As children, our parents forced us to go to bed early and rise early. Most times we rebelled because it was not comfortable, and we wanted to do what everyone was doing like watch TV and feel special. If there was something like a fast-forward button, we sure would press it, but nothing beats going through the process. As we grow, it becomes hard to catch up with everything because you know if you do not plan your day, life and activities, you end up losing out.

Your employers want you to resume work at a particular time. If you were super good, you would have more responsibilities on your plate. You might find it hard to even reach out to your parents and close friends because of the new responsibilities you have, and if you think being an entrepreneur exempts you from this, wait until you get the shocker.

Most entrepreneurs work 24 hours and do not even have resumption times. Anyone who tells you that they are their own "boss" and do not want anyone to control them could be living in a bubble. Have you done a great job and your client makes more demand for your product? Then you would figure out the reward for work is not rest, but more work. So, enjoy your youth, take life one step at a time, and prioritize your time well.

CHAPTER 8

A Stitch in Time Saves Nine

People often take this idiomatic expression for granted, using it mostly out of context. Let me put it in context: Procrastination is the thief of time. Not doing what you ought to do when you ought to do it is a sign of indiscipline.

One day, my dad was leaving for an event, so I saw him off to the car. As I headed back into the house, he beckoned on me and said, "You know you are about to write your WAEC Examination, it is wise for you to study hard and pass your examination in one sitting rather than have to retake it when your peers are already in the university. At that time it would be hard to focus because while they are taking university exams, you would still be taking WAEC exams". I heeded my father's advice, passed WAEC and gained admission into the University that same year.

While it is good to do things when our mates are doing it, we must also be careful about making the mistake of running ahead of time. We may be well suited for an opportunity but must wait for the appropriate time. Knowing when to act and when to stay put are very key decisions you need to make. You can learn more about time management and decision making by reading relevant books.

Insight

Be disciplined with your time, as timing is an important aspect of life. If you find that you're not able to meet up with someone at an agreed time, give them a heads up when you change your mind or when you're stuck, and don't be known as the person that doesn't keep to time. The best thing to do is to plan ahead for your appointments, and be in an hour before time. Make it a habit not to be the one that thinks there is something called "African time."

You would be rewarded more in business as a result of your punctuality and the way you spend your time. Don't be wasteful of it.

CHAPTER **9**

Three Magic Words:
Thank You, Please, I Am Sorry

These three words are magic keys that can open any door as long as it's the right lock. These three words used at the right time, in the right place and with the right people will unlock a door of endless pleasures and riches for you. As a married man, the most important word you can tell your wife is 'I'm sorry'. Women love to hear that word, it's more valuable than pricy gifts and jewelry because it reenacts and reaffirms your commitment to them.

In your daily commute, you could upset someone by mistake, even if it wasn't your fault, saying sorry can avert a lot of needless strife and squabbles. Sometimes you may be right, but must prove to be the stronger person by apologizing first. The same goes for saying Thank you. I buy items from a mall and when I pay and receive my items I say Thank you. For example, when it comes to using the word Please, you may want to obtain some important information from someone, you can simply put 'Please' before making such a request.

Saying 'Please' reaffirms your humility and expression of appreciation that the person is offering you a valuable service. There are bad days when they disappoint you, you should still not withhold the Thank you. Be grateful that people are willing to be of assistance to you – there are many people in dire need of advice and assistance who are hopelessly helpless.

Insight

Chivalry is almost a lost culture in the new era governed by technology and self-help routes. Technology gives us access to most things we take for granted. The effect of words on people and how much it shows us, I believe, makes it important for you to make courtesy a habit and a mantra.

Using these three words is not a weakness; rather, it is a sign of a well-cultured human and would always open doors for you in your personal life and the business world. It should be a lifestyle and not done at special moments. So how do you feel when people say 'Thank you, Please, or I am sorry'? I bet you feel great, so do all you can to make them your mantras, even on social media. It would be well worth it.

CHAPTER **10**

Humility Is Not Costly

There is a popular saying that goes thus: "Pride goes before a fall". One distinct thing worthy of note as a Nigerian is that Nigeria as a country (when I say country, I am insinuating its inhabitants) has a way of humbling you. There was a remarkable incident, where a billionaire was traveling by road and was stuck in traffic for hours. He had to call a private chopper to come to his aid and it did not stop tongues from wagging. Although our fingers are not equal as Nigerians, climate, topography and geography and not to mention the manmade hardship we have inflicted on ourselves, will teach you a bittersweet lesson.

Sometimes I think I'm strong and invincible. At other times, I feel weak and helpless. This has made me come to a decision to be humble, whether I am strong and invincible or weak and helpless. Reason being, when you are reigning, reign with wisdom because when the reign wears off, you still need people to support you so you don't hit rock bottom.

It is not easy to be humble in a country where money can buy everything and anyone. Nonetheless, a government can strip you of your wealth in one pronouncement. You might be driving the latest Mercedes Benz and a pothole will cost you your life; so be humble.

Insight

Growing up hearing the word humility, two things always come to mind before I worked on my mindset. First is selflessness and the second is shrinking my own light so people do not feel uncomfortable around me. There were several tweaks on my mind that changed everything for me.

Firstly we are all humans, and as fickle as that sounds, the best of us fall ill. We are mortals and can stop breathing the next moment and life would go on, no matter how loud, beautiful, handsome or highly successful we are. It's best to remind ourselves that we are living on borrowed time. This reminder helps to be humane to the next person, to be grounded and empathetic, to do better, to feel more grateful rather than getting carried away.

CHAPTER 11

Pay Now, Play Later

I cannot overemphasize this phrase. It is self-evident. In short, I have many instances of "delayed gratification" in my life that explain what I mean here. My mum always admonished me when I got back home on school holidays, to ignore girls and focus on my studies, when I start earning a living the girls would come. This sounded to me like gibberish, but I kept to it.

Truth be told: Before I got married, if my dad had not advised me to start my search for a wife at that stage of my life, I would have been very confused with my options (this is not me bragging but corroborating my mum's advice. She was actually right). Just imagine if I were dissipating the energy I needed to study on chasing girls up and down the place, I would have been another statistic. Thank God, that was not the case.

Another example was when I got back from the UK after my postgraduate studies; I started working with my dad at Complete Communications Limited. I walked to work and sometimes-used public transport. This went on for almost two years before my dad found me deserving of owning my own car.

There is a saying that goes thus; "all work and no play makes Jack a dull boy". This is relatively true, so as you work hard, find time to unwind so you do not have a nervous breakdown. Personally, I unwind by spending quality time with family and friends, eating out or visiting the park. In addition to that I work out at the gym to clear my head and de-stress.

Insight

We live in an era where everything is fast and quick; in essence a microwave generation. Fast food, fast life, you can even make an order for "fast friendships" and you sure would get it. The danger of this "fast everything" generation given to us because of technology is that, we sometimes forget what it feels like to wait and trust the process.

I believe that the more we grow, the more we figure out that not everything needs our energy; else, we major on the minor and minor on the major. There was a time when you had to hand-post letters and wait for some days to get it delivered to its destination, these days you would have to simply send an electronic mail and in seconds it would be received at the other end.

A school of thought believe this helped for delayed gratification. I liken it to the story of the prince who would be king but must everyday learn all he needs to prepare to be king. The goal of preparing him with books on the history of his .people, kings, and enemies of the state, is to help him when he assumes the throne. When you delay gratification and wait with purpose, you are better able to manage the pressure when your time comes. The best way to delay gratification is by going under authority, making yourself accountable to someone even when you have the power to be without one.

Young people who overcome peer pressure, normally stand a greater chance of overcoming life's challenges when they come knocking at any stage. Delayed gratification here includes: Putting aside today's pleasures in order to invest in tomorrow, to understand the process, to always ask the big questions such as 'how well does this serve me in the end'.

I believe the numbers and the 26 letters of the alphabet could have been taught to every child from the first day of birth but in the wisdom of our teachers they started with the number 1, 2, 3 and alphabets ABC because they understand the mind remembers in "threes". In addition, it gives the child time to get used to them.

The child normally with time handles the whole numbers and alphabets when he masters the basics.

In the real world, the things we are told to hold on to many times increase our decision-making skills. Living in Africa, our parents used stories to explain these acts of focusing on the first things first and it does count.

Some things to remind you of: You are not a fool if you do not have a boyfriend or girlfriend at your age, as long as you are also building healthy interpersonal relationships with the opposite sex. You are not a fool if you are not driving the latest car after secondary school or university.

You still have your years ahead of you to earn and buy cars. You are not a fool if all your friends are traveling abroad and it seems you can't even afford it, as long as you are busy developing yourself in your niche. In addition, the earlier you removed yourself from these pressures, the earlier and the more you develop the thick skin to live through life's bigger challenges.

CHAPTER 12

Readers Are Leaders

I started reading at a very tender age, my mom enforced a reading culture in my siblings and I. She encouraged us to read just about anything we could lay our hands on – pamphlets, billboards, posters, newspapers, magazines, etc. I have been reading consciously since I was 10 years old. Even though my school books were not particularly interesting, business books caught my interest. I was in love with reading about successful people and how they grew their wealth, it was a passion for me. And because of this, when I was leaving high school, I had written 3 proposals, which I shared with my dad.

During my first year in the university, taking the Entrepreneurial Development course, I did not have a problem coming up with a business idea because I already had three in my dad's custody. I was able to pass that course because I had an idea of how entrepreneurship worked even before coming to the university.

Whatever you want to be in life, some people have been there before you. Someone has done what you are planning to do, you can climb on their shoulders, no need to reinvent the wheel. It is only wise to go seek ideas and knowledge from them, some you cannot meet physically, but you can gain access to them by reading their books.

Insight

One of the best things reading does is the expansion of our minds to things and places we least imagine. The founder of Microsoft, Bill Gates and former president of the United States, Barack Obama have been global influencers, who make book reading a worthy challenge, as they both make it mandatory to share their reading list to their social media tribe. My first encounter with reading was newspapers, and then books which turned into a habit, thanks to my parents.

True readers are leaders; so when you read, read to find yourself approved and not just to make a point. We are the ones who will rewrite the narrative "Africans don't read." Obviously, with social media, it is getting more difficult these days to read even news stories and articles we come across online.

Many people simply read headlines and not the content, because it takes many muscles to read. The only way you lead people is by new knowledge, so go read a book on anything you fancy. That's a sure and fast way to gain other people's knowledge without having to meet them in person.

CHAPTER **13**

Choosing a Role Model

In my pre-teen years, I had role models. I doubt any teenager didn't have one. Those days, I admired the King of Pop Music - Michael Jackson (rest his soul), he was my role model. I loved the way he danced. His lyrics didn't make much sense to me then because I didn't bother to listen to what he was saying. I just sang along when it was chorus time. I could moon-walk, breakdance and while in High School, I used to woo the crowd with my dance moves on social nights. Michael Jackson was a big influence on my life.

As I grew older, I started to realize that life was more than just break dancing and girls telling you that you got great moves. You need to get a job and get a life, get married, you need to provide for your family and contribute meaningfully to your society. When this dawned on me, I started to research about people who I admire and are doing the things that I like, things that interest me. I started to read their books, attend their seminars when I could, and watch their biographies.

I have a long list of role models; Pastor Creflo Dollar, Sir Richard Branson, Kofi Annan (rest his soul), Olusegun Obasanjo, Bishop David Oyedepo, Pastor Robert Morris, Prince William, Donald Trump, Elon Musk, Barack Obama, Dr. Goodluck Jonathan and Nelson Mandela (rest his soul). I picked specific leadership attributes about them and studied them in that regard. They are all leaders and have different attributes that stand them out. Basically, I changed my mindset about role models after I saw the power a role model can potentially have on an individual's personal life. You can practically be exactly like them if you are crazy enough to walk in their path.

Insight

Because we crave influence and something to look forward to, it's always wise to be intentional about who we put in front of us as role models because they shape us. One way to always get this right is to question these moves when we get involved. So why are they my role models? What would I learn from them? Do their values align with mine? Am I confident to tell my future self this is why I am doing this? The role of role models is to help us have something in front of us to look forward to. Make sure your choices reflect your future self and not your current form because we keep evolving.

CHAPTER 14

Can't Do the Time, Don't Do the Crime

I learned this phrase while in High school. I do not know where I first heard it, but it resonated deeply with me. When I got in trouble in High school, I always looked down on the offense. I was always like "This is not a big deal, why are they punishing me". Now that I am older and know better, there is nothing like little offense, especially for a teenager. If you overlook the little offenses, they will grow up expecting you to overlook the big offenses.

One occasion that always comes to mind is, my Mom was always concerned about my dress sense. Growing up, it was fashionable to pop your collar, wear durag, wear your snap backs backward, and fly your shirt. She always complained anytime I was going out and questioned where I was going to. In my mind it was fashion, everyone was doing it, it was a harmless gesture, but I guess she just felt a decent person shouldn't be dressed in that manner. When I got into University I straightened out my dress sense as we were always reminded that how we dress is how we are addressed.

The catchphrase is as clear as it can be: if you do not want to be scolded or reprimanded, then don't go overboard. Growing up and knowing what I know now, all those offenses are actually big, and I will react the same way my teachers and parents reacted if I come by any teenager who flouts the rules. It is plain and self-explanatory, do not dabble into something if you know you are not ready to handle the consequences or later blame the devil. Do not compare yourself with anyone. That someone did it and got away with it, does not mean you will also get away with it.

Insight

My take is quite simple. You would always get the consequences of every action you take, and the dangers of making wrong choices at an early stage is that when you grow up, and attribute those choices to being young, society might find it hard to correct the already-established identity because it sure catches up on us fast. Life is in seasons, trust your intuition and understand some seasons can't be like the others, so be a student of yourself.

CHAPTER 15

Health Is Wealth

You must have heard severally that "your health is your wealth". This cannot be over-emphasized. When you decide to lead a healthy life, physically, mentally, socially, and nutritionally, you position yourself to tap into endless possibilities. This, however, is not a day's job; you have to continually work on yourself each day to be better.

For me, I exercise regularly. I have been health-conscious since High School. My friend and I gave ourselves targets when we went on long holidays to come back with six-packs, even though the reason was quite superficial. We had been told that the girls were attracted to 'packs', so we went all out through the long holidays depriving ourselves of all the sweets, chocolates and ice cream in order to resume school with six-packs.

Even though we had a superficial reason for going the healthy way, it had helped put us in great shape and now, after almost 17 years, my friend is still very fit. I cannot say that much about my muscularity, nonetheless, I am still very health-conscious and exercise regularly. We have been able to maintain a healthy mentality in every one of our endeavors. It's incredible how much little goals can become big achievements if you put your mind to it.

Insight

Training your body, mind, and spirit is also a form of exercise; deprivation can also be a form of mental exercise, likewise fasting. Watching what you eat and drink can help improve your overall health, and most importantly, maintaining a balanced life, is the key to lasting health and wealth.

As we grow older, we become less strong, and our bodies stop being as productive as they used to be, if we fail to exercise. The best way to keep up your health is not just to avoid toxic foods after exercising, but also to avoid toxic words and people, and be conscious of the things we feed our minds with.

CHAPTER 16

Be Your Own Competition

My mom always makes this statement "Only fools compare themselves with others". It always sounds quite harsh. I grew up being aware of the need to compete in school, in church, and at home, so it was strange to say people who compare themselves to others were fools; it sounded quite absurd.

When I was in University, I did not identify with any group, I was my own man. I did not try to be like the joneses, I put in check my desire to wear the latest outfits and shoes. I admired people who had them, but, I was not moved to desperation. I knew I had clothes and shoes that were great, they might not have been be the latest fashion, but they looked good on me.

Knowing what I know now, competition is an opportunist. It distorts your view of the world; it breeds jealousy and envy. Comparing yourself with other people is a precursor to depression. I really have not seen anyone who was content with their situation after comparing themselves with others. What competition does is to steal your joy and blind you from seeing what God has done for you, the gifts He has deposited in your life, and the destiny He has placed before you. Comparison gives you a false sense of worth and misplaced priority.

In order to live a purposeful life, we need to see ourselves as who we authentically are, the love God has got for us, all the good gifts He has bestowed upon us, looking at what we were yesterday, and how better we have improved today. Once you start to compare yourself with your own self, you will feel more confident that you can put to better use, those talents God has deposited in you. You will not be a copy, but a real image of yourself; you will feel self-worth and contentment.

Insight

No two humans are the same, and as we highlighted in the first chapter, the goal is always to understand self, be self-aware and understand our comparative advantage. I liken it to the analogy of the sun and the moon. The sun is the king of the day while the moon is the king of the night. The moon gets its light from the sun, but it uses it to brighten the night. All it does is wait for the night when the sun is done with its own cycle and it moves to be the light of the night.

Before we compare ourselves with others, its best we understand our comparative and competitive advantage and always bring them to bear in our life. Take your time to write out all that makes you unique and ask yourself what you can do with them at the end of this chapter.

You are a work in progress. Some of us never bloom until we are done with the university, some in secondary school, some peak at their elementary school; but in all be patient with you and be consistent in your growth and journey. Stop competing with people you should be collaborating with. And when it looks like you must compete, let it drive you to improve on yourself and be your best version.

There are two of football's greatest talents, Lionel Messi and Cristiano Ronaldo, who both played for the top football clubs in Spain at a time. Every time they stepped on the pitch, their fans kept comparing them to each other with regards to who was the greater. For over 15 years, they always emerged among the best in the world for any football award.

It was so funny that when one of them scores three goals in a match, it's seen as a wakeup call to the other. You are sure to get a response from the other the next time he plays during the week. Their football rivalry was and still remains the longest in the history of football because they both lived in the same era.

But by mid-2019, they both attended the UEFA award for the best football player. Journalists saw them talking like friends who had missed each other, and began to ask questions about what they feel about people comparing them. They both attested to the fact that they pushed each other to be better people. The lesson here is that if your competition does not help you be a better version of yourself, then you sure must rethink it. In the end, it's about how eager you are to improve yourself than how eager you are to be like the other person.

CHAPTER 17

Winning Against Depression and Mental Health Issues

We live in a generation where we want everything fast and on-demand. It can get a bit overwhelming. Social media adds to this by making us feel like we do not need to work hard to achieve anything worth celebrating, like we can sleep and wake up a billionaire the next morning. You see your friends going on expensive vacations, wearing expensive human hair, using designer and luxury items, and you wonder why God hates you so much. God does not hate you; He put those people in your life to motivate you.

Depression is an opportunist and its twin sibling is unhealthy comparison. Once you start comparing yourself with others, you will unconsciously open the door to depression. It's rather sad that people rely on social media for validation rather than building healthy relationships in real life. Some of the things you see posted on social media are not a reflection of reality. Again, no one posts their failures on social media and it only takes a courageous person to post their failures on social media in order to educate others.

While some people might be battling depression because of the trends in these new times, some others actually suffer from depression because of their genetic make-up. Some cases of depression might not be because of social media, comparison or other difficult times people are experiencing in their life but as a result of the genetic make-up of such people. For example, if your temperament is melancholy you are likely to be prone to mood swings, worry, anxiety or depression. You can find books on temperament and mental health and learn more.

For people who worry a lot, it's important to remember that 99% of the things we worry about do not happen. It is hard to keep a positive outlook always; however, learn to always show up, even if you don't feel like it. In addition, affirming positive words like "I can do all things through Christ who strengthens me", "The Lord shall supply all my needs according to His riches in glory", can bring you out of depression. It is also strongly suggested that people seek medical help by seeing a doctor or a psychologist when they feel depressed or become suicidal because depression as a mental illness can be treated medically.

For example, in Nigeria, there are a growing number of mental health specialists, one of which is Mentally Aware Nigeria Initiative (MANI). Furthermore, the kind of environment we find ourselves, the relationships we keep, the kinds of thoughts we let our minds process, and the kind of information we fill our minds with overtime, will take us out of depression or get us into depression.

Insight

Research suggests that we have more young people likely to fall into depression in this era, compared to other generations. Some of the reasons highlighted include excess consumption of social media and a comparison culture. The big question is: Why has the number of suicide and depression cases risen today compared to years before? I believe there was little room for comparison then.

These days the "in your face" distractions we have around us, is like going to the grocery store to find different brands of a product on the shelf. It takes a high level of discipline to refuse the others and pick the one you came for.

The comparison culture among young people, and the choice of trying to be someone they are not, is the newest generational challenge.

This has led to several mental challenges, one of which is suicide. If you fail at anything, always re-member that failure is a form of feedback and not a sign that you are not good enough. Whenever you think you are less than you are, or that life is not worth it, remind yourself that your thought might be right at that point in time, but do well not to make permanent decisions over some irrational thought. Remember, if you commit suicide, besides ending a possibly bright future, you can create more problems for the ones you leave behind. Your siblings, your parents, and your friends may become scarred in ways they might not recover from.

So, let us have a deal: whenever you get suicidal thoughts or start behaving irrationally, find someone you trust and whom you know wants you to suc-ceed, and share with them just how you feel. This will make you feel better. If you live in Nigeria, there are a number of suicide emergency hotlines in parts of the country.

We need you alive to see the end of this journey. No matter how hard it gets, do not give up on life. Practice self-care, reach out to someone you trust, and keep living life – one step at a time.

CHAPTER 18

Evil Communication Corrupts Absolutely

When we talk about corruption, many people's thoughts go to being unfaithful with money, not being able to handle money, and stealing the nation's wealth. While this may be true, it is not the only definition of corruption.

Corruption, as defined by the Webster Dictionary, is "a departure from the original or from what is pure or correct". This definition of corruption is not only limited to government officials or powerful people. Corruption prevents you from attaining your true potential. When you hang around the wrong people, wrong information, and the wrong environment, they will surely affect your outlook on life and the way you interpret, analyze, and synthesize information. The kind of information you have available to you will determine the kind of life you will live.

Hence, when you mingle with the wrong crowd, it corrupts your identity. Your goal is to be salt and light to your family, friends, and nation. Salt gives taste, which is value, while light brings direction, which means honor to your family, friends, and nation. You must strive to always be around the right crowd, the people who inspire you to be better than you were yesterday.

By this, we do not mean to be in competition with people but to compliment others, to excel with positive values and standards that birth a healthy lifestyle. This will bring great benefits to you and to those who come in contact with you. You should be a magnet for good things, and this is only possible when you have the right network of people and information around you.

Insight

Someone once tried explaining corruption with this analogy. You walk into a room with swords, you were told corruption lives there. With anger, you brandish your sword and swear to destroy everyone. The door shuts on you only to lift your sword to the right and figure out the face is a familiar one, so you drop your sword. Looking to your left, the face you see shocks you.

The more you walk, the more you figure out that

everyone in the room you least expect is corrupt and resides there.

Your sword falls off your hand, the door opens and you walk out more depressed than you were when you came in. Only then do you figure out you need to be careful of who is in your circle and the cause you support, because, in the end, you might only be living in your own bubble.

Be conscious of yourself first, and your circle of influence, because, in as much as you think nothing moves you, your circle of influence and your decisions can ruin your chances at life.

Tending to Your Finances

My siblings and I grew up with a wooden spoon, graduated to plastic, bronze, and eventually silver spoons.
When you ask a young person why he or she is not
able to implement their business ideas, they quickly
reply that they lack the necessary capital to start the
business. While this may hold true in some cases, it
does not reflect the true picture in most cases. I will
not go deep into this, as many books have already
dealt with this challenge.

However, in summary, what he/she lacks is a winning
mentality. Even the biblical Jesus who had no business
investments, never lacked resources when he needed it the most. A good account was when Jesus was
asked to pay tax. Although he had no business nor
was gainfully employed, he simply instructed Peter to
get money from the mouth of a fish.

This illustration trumps the fact that you need capital to start and run your business. In my opinion, the only thing you need capital for, is when you want to scale your business. There is a principle I want to share with you on how to manage your finances. It's called the 10% principle. It states that 10% of your earnings go to God as tithe, another 10% goes to your savings, and then 10% to investments. You are left with 70%, which might be enough to solve your problems. The reason I said might solve your problems is; God has promised us He will not allow us to be tempted much more than we can bear.

One common mistake people make is; they pay their tithe as offering or give it to charity. These kinds of giving should come from your remaining 70%. The 10% is for God and He is a jealous God. He does not share His glory with anybody. In addition, for those who say they do not have money to tithe: Did you wake up this morning? If your answer is "YES" then you can pay 2.4 hours of your day as tithe to God either by meditation, volunteering to causes you are passionate about, taking time to counsel people who are challenged or helping people in need in your own little way.

The reason I am particular about tithing is because, the 10% makes the remaining 90% useful for you. It takes discipline to religiously do this and one thing is constant, if you can straighten out your finances, every other aspect of your life will align. Then you will see things going for you in the right direction.

Insight

Some of the basic things you must learn with regards to life, health and money include: How compound interest works, why drinking water compared to soda is advisable daily and how much healthier it is, how not eating outside can save you much money, why cooking should be a life skill on your must-learn skills list, especially for men (it's a survival skill).

It's also important to learn why having more than one account (one for savings and the other for spending) normally works, or why leaving a standing order for your bank to deduct some money from it monthly normally works, why having a pension scheme early in your twenties, as long as you start earning, is not luxury, etc. In all these, the positives here is in what we become in the end by practicing the above. If you are disciplined and are able to manage your income and finance in this way early enough, you will be way ahead in the game of life, and we want you to be way ahead.

A couple of years ago, I started producing my TV show which featured young people making business impact. I've been honoured to notice some consistent, young and smart entrepreneurs, who have turned business friends. One of them helps solve the problems with regards savings by creating a savings platform. One saving platform I highly recommend is PiggyVest, formally known as Piggy Bank.

At the time of this writing, I've introduced about seven young people who found it hard to save their money, who started saving with the app and are now proud of what they can do for themselves with it. The issue of finance should be taken seriously because among every other thing, it is still one of the reasons for the high rate of divorce in young marriages. Money has always been a tool; so, start early to make use of it as a tool. The goal of this heads-up on finance is to help you become more financially aware on your journey, and that you act on them and ace your game.

CHAPTER **20**

Choosing a Life Partner

Choosing a life partner is one of the most important decisions you would ever make. Failing to make the right choice of spouse is irredeemable; it only takes the grace of God to get back on track and even at that, the scars are with you forever. I met my wife on Mark Zuckerberg's social media platform, Facebook. Even though I had learned a bit about her, the first time I set my eyes on her was when we had a New Year celebration at my family house. It was a yearly event for family bonding and camaraderie. In this convivial atmosphere, unknown to me, my mom had invited her and her siblings to join us that year. Obviously, my mother had harmlessly invited her friend's daughters to attend our family hangout (this was my assumption).

We eventually got talking that day and we clicked. Even though we had been chatting on Facebook, I did not make a concrete decision about her nor my intentions. I got her number that day, and that was the beginning of getting to know each other better. Our marriage has had a lot of "topsy turvy" moments, but because we truly love each other, we have found a way to continue to grow in love, even though we are not totally compatible (what the love shrinks call irreconcilable differences).

The moment I started to realize that this lady was created by God, in His image, and it was I who signed the dotted lines, wore the traditional attire, and went to church to consummate the holy matrimony, I started to value our union. To top it up, God in his infinite mercies blessed us with a beautiful girl as our first child who has made our bond even stronger. Marriage is about making compromises and taking responsibility. These two characteristics with a little growing up on my part, have proven to be the spice of our marriage. I love my wife and I put my family first.

No one can choose a life partner for you. If you allow it, it can lead to situations that will threaten the very essence of the marriage. In addition to this, one of my mentors on one occasion asked my wife and I a pertinent question before our wedding. His question was: "What was your motive for marrying this Man/ Woman?" We both responded, and he admonished us to never forget the reason why we decided to be together. In addition, whenever you feel let down or slighted in the relationship, always remember your reasons for saying "I do".

Insight

Depending on when you are reading this book, the media is always awash of stories of failed marriages, which on its own has handed marriage a bad name, and subtly sent fear waves onto this generation. Marriage is two people telling each other that although they are different and have their own flaws, but because of the things they both believe and agree to daily work on, the things that bind them become more than the things that divide them. In addition, both should acknowledge every compromise they make.

In case you have given up on marriage because of societal perceptions or observations, I believe we can give it all the attention we give to other things like school and work; meaning that we should always invest time in how it works and those it is working for, rather than citing instances of where it has failed. Let us not label the institution, but prepare to give it our best shot as we do our careers. And when we have a breakdown, we should be humble enough to go to those who would be truthful to us. I believe there is really no one formula for a successful marriage but the more exposed we are to what works, the earlier we are equipped for our own journey.

Bonus Chapter: Honor Your Parents

I will address the parents first, because it would be unfair to admonish teenagers and young adults born in the social media era, without first admonishing their parents on the need to bring up the child in the right principles so when they grow up, they will not depart from it.

With that introduction, I believe that children of this new era are very intelligent, as they are fondly called Millennials and Generation Z. The Millennials built the technology, whereas Generation Z grew up to meet technology. With the generation that built the technology, there is a craze to be followed, liked and appreciated for looks, toys, gadgets, appearance, and although absurd, nudity.

While all these are not very bad things in themselves, they are unhealthy, just for the simple fact that obsession can lead to depression/ oppression. Many teenagers and youths have committed suicide because of the false information they consumed on social media. To really drive home my point, you would need to refer to chapters 2, 5, and 6 of this book. Not everyone had the privilege I had, growing up with a caring dad and mom, though there are numerous stories of people who still came out unscathed despite being orphans. My dad is a worthy example.

This singular reason was my justification for naming this chapter a bonus, because it is a gift from God to have parents who love you, advise you, and give you godly counsel, not to mention the financial support through the years. Repaying them will be utopian, that is why the Bible reminds us to honor our father and mother so that our days would be long – this is the only commandment with a promise.

So, whatever your parents have done or not done for you, know that having both of your parents alive is a bonus and a blessing. I pray that God will open your eyes to see the desires of your parents' hearts and grant you the resources to honor them, Amen.

Insight

The biggest new threat to making connections among humans, is digital technologies and gadgets. We live, eat, and sleep with our phones and gadgets, with several numbers of phony friends on social media and the illusion that we are happy, while seeking the validation of strangers. There have been more suicide rates globally as a result of over-reliance on technology, in place of having human connection with friends and family.

As we grow up and leave our families, besides sending them money when necessary, we should not forget the place of quality time. We must have 'family time' where we intentionally share quality time with loved ones, especially our parents. This is the best kind of honour they require in their old age.

Nuggets of Wisdom by Solomon Ojeagbase

- Be a man of many principles but few rules. To live in peace with people you have to be flexible with rules. A lot of people have more rules than principles which leads to egotism and false self-image.

- When it feels like the weight of the world is on your shoulder, you can't stand tall and your face looks to the ground, remember, the journey of a thousand miles begins with a step. Victory only goes to those who don't quit. You have come this far now to give up, keep hope alive with your eyes on the crown with a star. Those who backed down had the time of grace but never got the chance to claim the prize. To quit is a choice not the only option, you can pick yourself up even though you fall seven times. The blood in your veins, air in your lungs, and a pounding heart should give you the assurance that if you don't quit the race, your reward is guaranteed.

- When you spend time with people, you give them a piece of your mind. When you invest time with people, you grant them unwavering access to your heart. Wisdom demands you discern between the two as the heart is the window to the soul. Therefore invest time with people who nourish your soul.

- The reward for Investing in people cannot be quantified as there is no limit to what man can give/ achieve. Inversely the investment in any financial instrument can be measured therefore is in ad finitum.

- Assumption is the currency of fools only tenable in the market of ignorance

- If you have Vision, Drive and Passion, no force on earth can stop you. However you will need Patience, Courage and Faith to make the impossible possible

- Give your heart to love and you'll experience love without limit. Give your heart to hate and you'll wish you never did. To experience love let your heart always be filled with love.

- When you are not content with who you are, you try to be someone else. When you fail at trying, you get jealous of the person. Jealousy becomes envy when you lose sight of your uniqueness and fail in trying to become someone else. Envy becomes hate when you realize you have spent a good deal of time chasing shadows. Hate in your mind breeds evil machinations that can lead to the cruelest deeds. It all started from discontentment which untamed became full blown resentment.

- Live life, be grateful and thankful. An attitude of gratitude always precedes a higher altitude.

- Be ye not one who waits in vain. Take heed for life's events will overtake you. Do what you can while you still can 'cos brethren, patience has a deadline.

- Money is shy and timid, just like a love affair, she needs to be courted and cultivated. Riches come to those who desire it and make demands of her. On the contrary poverty is bold and ruthless. Poverty needs no invitation, futile expectations and procrastination opens wide the door.

- The terms Suffering and Sacrifice are often misused interchangeably, the latter has a price tag and a reward, and also there is an end in sight. The former however is an indefinite sentence to a life of pain without restitution.

- With money you can get whatever you want. Subsequently the quality or quantity of what you get is dependent on how much money you have.

- Countless people have imbibed the erroneous habit of planning and scheming while a few have developed a penchant for execution. In the end, the planners become baffled and dismayed when they see their plans being beautifully engendered by those who execute. Plan with the end in mind, while at it hold your work tools.

- To live a purpose driven life, Men ought to be GODMade and SelfMotivated rather than be SelfMade and MoneyMotivated

- Standing alone doesn't mean I am alone, it means I am strong enough to handle things all by myself.

- My confession is devoid of E.G.O (Edging God Out) rather an acknowledgement of the truth that I am Godmade and SelfMotivated

- To be an effective leader, you must rule with even handedness. All fingers are not equal but they are part of the hand

- If you feel life is unfair, try holding your breath for 1 (one) minute. That sinking feeling you get is what separates those who win from those who quit.

- In school they teach you to read through the lines, on the streets they teach you to read between the lines. Acquire both street and book smart and you will be unstoppable

- A life without love, is like a life without a thumb. You can hold nothing.

- I beseech thee brethren tempt not, neither bear ye false witness against another. Judge not for the Lord knows those whose hearts are stayed on Him. Be ye not one who tempts his brother so you can say he is this or he is that. For I have made a covenant of grace with every man under the sun. The intentions of a man's heart are made known by his words and through his actions his desires are made manifest.

- God gives us two choices to make; good and bad. Man gives you only bad choices, if you choose less bad you are guilty, if you choose greater bad you are guilty. If you don't choose at all you are a pretender so still guilty. Let people be comfortable doing good without drawing any cynical or oxymoronic inferences. In so doing, good will permeate the hearts of men and people will naturally eschew evil. Give someone a chance to do good today.

- It's doesn't matter what people say, perceive or insinuate about you. Because, the truth comes from within and can only be seen when you look in the mirror. When you know yourself, what people think can't define you. It may slow you down but cannot disqualify you.

- My opinion is the sum total of my experiences, religious beliefs, emotions and relationships. What I think should in no way stop you from having your own opinion. It's the way I see life, it doesn't mean I hate you or think any less of you. And I will in no way treat you based on sentiments but it's good for me to let you know where I stand on some issues and it's is your duty to not get offended or infuriated. If everyone left earth and lived in the sky there would still be room enough for more people. That is how opinion works, you can have an opinion about a subject so long it does not put people in harm's way physically, psychologically or emotionally economically more importantly does not deprive them of the benefits of being human. Don't impose your opinion on others or make them feel worse off because they don't see things your way. We can still live together in peace if we both understand that depending on where we stand 6 and 9 are both correct and is just a matter of our differing perspectives.

- Many Christians juxtapose Grace with work. You don't pray for Gods leading without first having an idea to be led on. You have to go through the mental rigors of thinking. You cannot pray for rain when you have not first planted a seed. The latter precedes the former.

- Vision; that is the basic qualification for any leader. Ability to look into the future then plan

- Nigeria needs visionary leaders not academic scholars

- The more you are thankful, the more your barns are full.

- Money is the essence of life, it is the salt to the soup of life. Without money life will be tasteless

- To succeed at anything in life, begin with the end in mind, then reverse engineer.

Reading Recommendations

How to make it in Nigeria: Building your wealth from ground floor up - Dr. Sunny Emmanuel Ojeagbase

How to bullet proof yourself from poverty - Dr. Sunny Emmanuel Ojeagbase

Ideas - The starting point of all true Riches - Dr. Sunny Emmanuel Ojeagbase

What they don't teach you at Lagos Business School - Dr. Sunny Emmanuel Ojeagbase

Learn it! Do it! Sell it! - Dr. Sunny Emmanuel Ojeagbase

All you need to know to have all your needs met - Bishop David Oyedepo

Understanding prosperity - Bishop David Oyedepo

Towards Mental Exploits - Bishop David Oyedepo

Following the path of the Eagle - Bishop David Oyedepo

Possessing your possession - Bishop David Oyedepo

You can if you think you can - Norman Vincent Pearle

Battlefield of the mind - Joyce Meyer

Losing my Virginity - Richard Branson

Jewish wisdom for business Success - Rabbi Levi Brackman and Sam Jaffe

The Art of the deal - Donald J. Trump

Think and Grow Rich - Napoleon Hill

The richest Man in Babylon - George S. Clason

Rich Dad, Poor Dad - Robert Kiyosaki

Purpose driven Life - Rick Warren

The Alchemist - Paolo Cohelo

David and Goliath - Malcom Gladwell.

Breaking the Coconut - Charles Umeh

About the Authors

Solomon Ojeagbase was born in the capital city of Lagos State, Ikeja. He is a graduate of Covenant University where he studied for a BSc. in International Relations. He also has an MBA from the prestigious Lagos Business School.

In 2016, he was nominated for Professional Service at The Future Awards Africa for his contribution to the development of the digital football community on-line, through Complete Sports website and other digital communities which he built from ground up.

He regards himself as a Hybrid Manager, whose work has received much deserved critical acclaim, with honours as Top Sports Blog in Africa at the 2016 African Blogger Awards awarded by Webfluential, Business Insight Award for Most Innovative Premier League News Provider 2018/2019 (Nigeria), Business

Excellence award as Nigeria's Best Daily Sports Website for 2019/2020 awarded by Acquisition International (AI) amongst others.

He is the convener of Complete Sports Celebrity Workout a physical and mental fitness event. Which he created to not only foster healthy living through exercising, but to also bring to our consciousness the importance of exercise, while educating us about the benefits of doing so.

He isn't just a sports head, he also volunteers his time and expertise to speaking at conferences like Social Media Week (Lagos), civic and charity events. He still has a passion for International Relations as he occasionally attends MUN conferences globally.

You can reach him on social media @tosinbranson on Twitter and Instagram.

Charles Umeh is a TED Speaker an International published Author, and business Coach. Born in the city of Lagos, Nigeria. He also serves as a management Consultant, and host the B.T.C (Breaking The Coconut) TV Show. Which gives us insights into lessons entrepreneurs and change makers face in Africa.

His first book BREAKING THE COCONUT, tells the stories of African Millennials, Change Agents and their capacity to beat life's odds. His book, is available in

over 38,000 online bookstores globally and on www.
breakingthecoconut.com. His TV show is watched all
over Nigeria. .

Charles leads the Breaking The Coconut INC team. A
next generation research and knowledge media firm
in Africa whose work put the spotlight on educating
the next generation for the evolving future of work.

With the breaking, the coconut show broadcast
among top media outfits in Africa. While "the coconut
worklab" a collaborative learning and development
platform collaborate with entrepreneurs and stake-
holders in the workplace with knowledge and skills
for the future of work. His work focuses on the generation next in the workplace.

CPSIA information can be obtained
at www.ICGtesting.com
Printed in the USA
LVHW091231171220
674414LV00005B/829